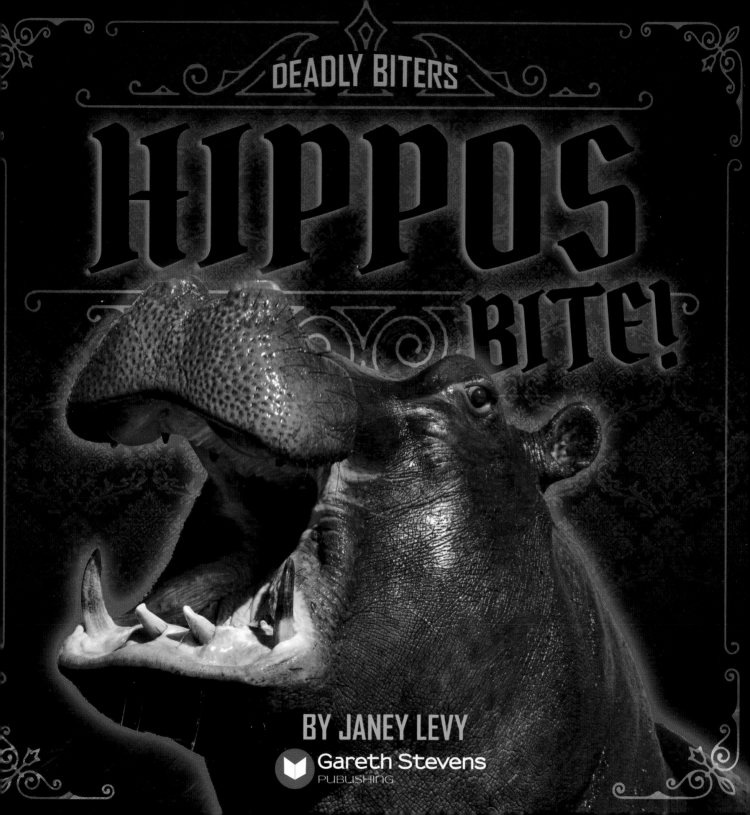

DEADLY BITERS

HIPPOS BITE!

BY JANEY LEVY

Gareth Stevens
PUBLISHING

Please visit our website, www.garethstevens.com. For a free color catalog of all our high-quality books, call toll free 1-800-542-2595 or fax 1-877-542-2596.

Library of Congress Cataloging-in-Publication Data

Names: Levy, Janey, author.
Title: Hippos bite! / Janey Levy.
Description: New York : Gareth Stevens Publishing, [2021] | Series: Deadly biters | Includes index.
Identifiers: LCCN 2020000853 | ISBN 9781538257760 (library binding) | ISBN 9781538257746 (paperback) | ISBN 9781538257753 (6 Pack) | ISBN 9781538257777 (ebook)
Subjects: LCSH: Hippopotamus--Juvenile literature.
Classification: LCC QL737.U57 L483 2021 | DDC 599.63/5--dc23
LC record available at https://lccn.loc.gov/2020000853

First Edition

Published in 2021 by
Gareth Stevens Publishing
111 East 14th Street, Suite 349
New York, NY 10003

Copyright © 2021 Gareth Stevens Publishing

Designer: Reann Nye
Editor: Meta Manchester

Photo credits: Cover, p. 1 pjmalsbury/E+/Getty Images; cover, pp. 1-24 (background) Reinhold Leitner/Shutterstock.com; p. 5 Paul Souders/Stone/Getty Images; p. 7 Peter Hermes Furian/Shutterstock.com; p. 9 John Carnemolla/Corbis Documentary/Getty Images; p. 11 Marc Dumont/Shutterstock.com; p. 12 Elliotte Rusty Harold/Shutterstock.com; p. 13 Vittorio Ricci - Italy/Moment/ Getty Images; p. 14 Karel Bartik/Shutterstock.com; p. 15 Sren Pedersen /EyeEm/Getty Images; p. 16 PhotocechCZ/ Shutterstock.com; p. 17 Gerrit_de_Vries/Shutterstock.com; p. 19 Paul A. Souders/Stone/Getty Images; p. 21 ac productions/Getty Images.

Printed in the United States of America

Some of the images in this book illustrate individuals who are models. The depictions do not imply actual situations or events.

CPSIA compliance information: Batch #CS20GS: For further information contact Gareth Stevens, New York, New York at 1-800-542-2595.

Find us on 🅕 🅸

CONTENTS

Words in the glossary appear in **bold** type
the first time they are used in the text.

HELLO HIPPO!

Perhaps you've read a storybook about hippos or seen one at a zoo. Their features make them seem almost cute. They have a large, round body with short, fat legs and a giant head. They're usually herbivores, or plant eaters, so they don't seem scary. But hippos are some of Africa's most feared animals.

Hippos are **aggressive** and dangerous. Their huge mouth holds some sharp teeth, and their bite is powerful. Inside this book, you'll discover lots more about hippos and their bite.

CHEW ON THIS!

When hippos fight each other, they even use their giant head as a **weapon**!

"Hippopotamus" comes from a Greek word meaning "river horse." Hippos don't look like horses, and they aren't actually **related** to them.

HIPPOS' HOME AND HABITAT

You might have seen hippos at a zoo. But if you want to see them in the wild, you'll have to travel to Africa. Long ago, hippos were found in Europe and Asia. But **climate** changes and human hunting killed their populations in these areas. Today, the common or large hippo only lives south of the Sahara Desert in Africa. Another smaller kind, the pygmy hippo, lives in West Africa.

Hippos like a certain kind of **habitat**. They live in slow-moving rivers and lakes that have grasslands around them.

CHEW ON THIS!

Hippos used to be common along the Nile River in Egypt, in northern Africa. However, they're **extinct** there now.

WHERE HIPPOS LIVE TODAY

SAHARA DESERT

AFRICA

■ HIPPO TERRITORY

Here are the places you can see hippos
in the wild today.

HIPPOS' HUGE BODIES

Hippos are *huge* animals. They can be up to 16.5 feet (5 m) long and stand 5.2 feet (1.6 m) tall at the shoulder. Females weigh about 3,000 pounds (1,361 kg). Males can weigh up to 9,920 pounds (4,500 kg). That's more than a pickup truck!

Hippos are grayish-brown, with a pink stomach and pink around their mouth, eyes, and ears. Although they're **mammals**, they have very little hair. But they do have stiff hairs on their upper lip and tail.

CHEW ON THIS!

An old tale said that hippos sweat blood. The truth is that their skin gives off an oily reddish matter that keeps it safe from the sun.

A hippo's mouth is almost 20 inches (0.5 m) wide!

9

ADAPTED FOR AQUATIC LIFE

Did you know hippos spend up to 16 hours a day in the water? Because of that, they have special **adaptations** for life in the water.

Hippos' ears, eyes, and nose are high on their head so they stay above the water while the rest of the body is under the water. When hippos are completely under the water, their ears and nose shut to keep water out. A thin, clear covering keeps their eyes safe and still lets hippos see.

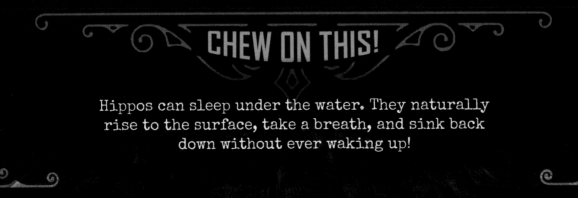

CHEW ON THIS!

Hippos can sleep under the water. They naturally rise to the surface, take a breath, and sink back down without ever waking up!

Hippos can hold their breath for 5 minutes or more when they're under the water.

BLOATS AND BABIES

Hippos are social animals that live in groups. Those groups are known by many different names: herd, bloat, pod, siege, or school. The leader is the most powerful male. He's the one that gets to **mate** with the adult females in his group.

Eight months after mating, a female has one baby that weighs almost 100 pounds (45.4 kg)! Baby hippos start to eat grass when they're about 1 month old, but continue to nurse until they're 6 to 8 months old.

CHEW ON THIS!

A baby hippo may be born on land or in the water.

Bloats are usually 10 to 30 animals. But they may be as large as 200 animals!

FEARFUL BITE FORCE

Hippos can open their mouth very wide and bite down with great force. Their bite force is 1,800 pounds per square inch (126.6 kg per sq cm). That's stronger than the bite of a polar bear! And hippos have long, sharp teeth at the front of their mouth that make the bite worse.

If hippos are mostly herbivores, why do they need a powerful bite and long, sharp teeth? Males use them when they fight other males. They're also used against enemies.

CHEW ON THIS!

A hippo's bite force is powerful enough to squash a crocodile—a mighty predator—or to break a boat!

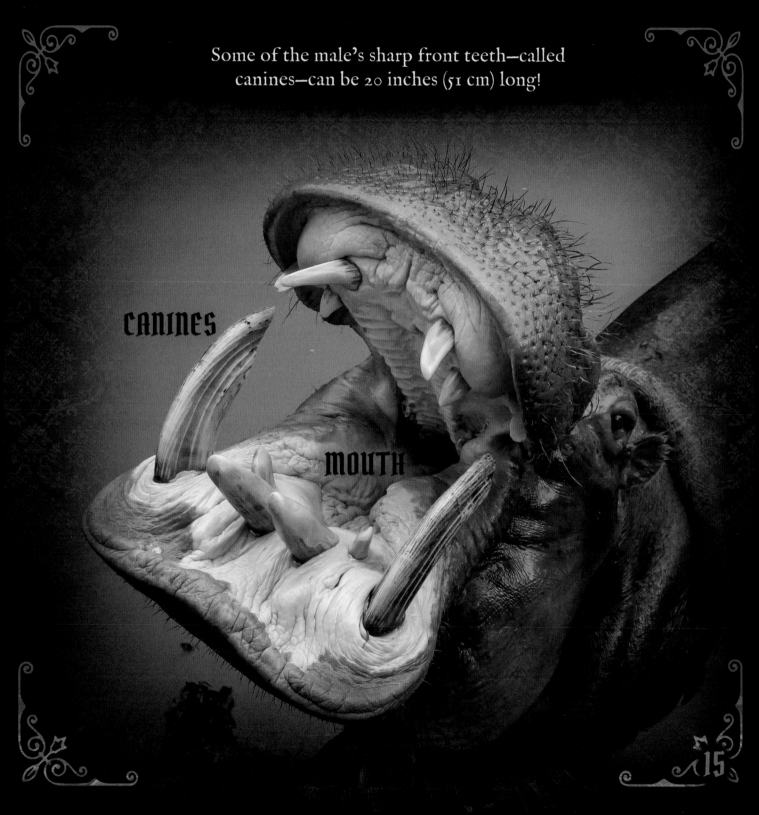

Some of the male's sharp front teeth—called canines—can be 20 inches (51 cm) long!

CANINES

MOUTH

BEASTLY BATTLES

Why do male hippos fight each other? They fight over areas of land and the right to mate with females. They usually start by sizing each other up. The males stand nose to nose, each opening his mouth as wide as possible. Usually the smaller male just leaves. If he doesn't, a terrible fight follows.

The males roar and rip with their sharp teeth. They even swing their huge heads like a hammer! Males can be badly hurt or even killed in these fights.

CHEW ON THIS!

Scientists saw one hippo fight that started when a young male bit the tail off an old male! Ouch!

This first stage of a hippo fight is called gaping.

HIPPOS AND HUMANS

Hippos aren't just dangerous to each other and their enemies, such as crocodiles, lions, and hyenas. They're dangerous to people too! They have powerful weapons to use, they're aggressive, and they guard their territory. It's believed hippos kill about 500 people each year!

But people are dangerous to hippos too. They take the water hippos need and use it for crops. People hunt hippos for food and for their teeth. They take over hippos' habitats, so hippos don't have as many places to live.

CHEW ON THIS!

It doesn't look like it, but hippos can run fast. They can run up to 30 miles (48 km) per hour!

Hippo teeth are made of ivory, like elephant **tusks** are, however hippo ivory is a bit softer. Both types of ivory are illegal for most people to have.

HIPPOS HELP THEIR ECOSYSTEM

Hippos may be dangerous, but they are important to their **ecosystem**. They poop a lot during their hours in the water, and many kinds of fish eat their poop.

The hippos' poop also has matter called silicon, which is needed by tiny plantlike living things called algae that live in water. Those algae form the basis of the **food chain** in many water ecosystems. That means hippos and their poop make life possible in these lakes and rivers!

CHEW ON THIS!

Scientists consider hippo populations vulnerable, or in some danger of dying out. That means there's a lot of danger for their ecosystems as well.

Fish also eat little creatures that live on the hippos' skin.

GLOSSARY

adaptation: a change in a type of animal that makes it better able to live in its surroundings

aggressive: showing a readiness to attack

climate: the average weather conditions of a place over a period of time

ecosystem: all the living things in an area

extinct: no longer living

food chain: a series of organisms in which one uses the next lowest one as food

habitat: the natural place where an animal or plant lives

mammal: a warm-blooded animal that has a backbone and hair, breathes air, and feeds milk to its young

mate: to come together to make babies

related: two people or animals connected by family

tusk: a large tooth that curves up and out of an animal's mouth

weapon: something used to fight an enemy

FOR MORE INFORMATION

BOOKS

Heos, Bridget. *Do You Really Want to Meet a Hippopotamus?* Mankato, MN: Amicus High Interest, 2017.

Maynard, Thane. *Saving Fiona: The Story of the World's Most Famous Baby Hippo.* New York, NY: Houghton Mifflin Harcourt Publishing, 2018.

Riggs, Kate. *Hippopotamuses.* Mankato, MN: Creative Education, 2016.

WEBSITES

Hippopotamus
kids.nationalgeographic.com/animals/mammals/hippopotamus/
Read more about hippos here, see some photos, and watch an awesome video.

How Hungry Are Hippos?
www.wonderopolis.org/wonder/how-hungry-are-hippos
Learn more facts about hippos here and check out some fun activities to do with friends and family.

World's Deadliest: Hippo vs. Hippo
video.nationalgeographic.com/video/worlds-deadliest/00000144-0a3f-d3cb-a96c-7b3f7e880000
Watch a video of two male hippos fighting over territory and mates on this website.

INDEX